Steps to Financial Peace of Mind

Move from Information Overload
to a Focused Plan and
Feel Good about Your Future

Charles Brophy

 Perissos Media

Published by
Perissos Media
www.PerissosMedia.com

ISBN-13: 9781515391302
ISBN-10: 1515391302

To arrange a consultation that could change your life and financial future, take the next step and contact Charles using the details below:

Brophy Financial Planning
106-99 Holland Avenue
Ottawa, ON K1Y 0Y1 Canada
Phone: 613-728-9573
Toll free: 1-800-288-1263
e-mail: charlie@brophyfinancial.com
www.brophyfinancial.com

CONTENTS

INTRODUCTION

My first lesson about inflation and economics came from my father. He was born in 1905, married my mother when he was 43 years old, and raised eight children on the family farm where I now reside.

Together with his brothers, my father left his farm in the Ottawa Valley in 1925 to work for Henry Ford in Detroit. He made $1,000 a year.

Back then, he could buy a new Ford Model A for about $500 or six months of wages. He could also purchase a modest home in the area for about $5,000 or five years of wages.

Our father used to tell us that the ratios between product and price couldn't change because otherwise the working person wouldn't be able to afford a car or a home; either the wages would have to rise or the prices would have to drop.

Fast-forward to today. A young person fresh out of university or a trade school could expect to earn about $50,000 annually. He could expect to purchase a new vehicle for about $25,000 or six months of wages and a modest home for about $250,000 or five years of wages.

The world has changed a lot over the past 90 years, but some things have remained remarkably constant. My father was right: inflation might add a few zeros to prices, but the ratios stay about the same.

It's a volatile, fast-paced world out there. A lot can change in the blink of an eye, and in the world of investments, that blink can mean the difference between retiring in comfort and just scraping by.

Everywhere we look these days, we are being bombarded with all kinds of financial information. We are being overloaded with the latest financial trend or fad, promises of sky-high returns and no-risk investments.

The promise of success and financial security—with minimal effort and risk—can lure the uninformed to make poor decisions.

But with everyone from your best friend to your

next-door neighbor offering you financial advice, it can be hard to know whom to trust.

I have been in the financial industry for more than 30 years and my team and I have seen plenty of fads come and go. We believe that even in this whirlwind day and age, some things never change: there is value in investing, it is important to diversify your portfolio, and it is wise to choose investments that are in line with your profile.

We have proudly built our business on offering our clients sound financial advice based solidly on tried-and-true principles. We listen closely to our clients to understand their motivations, their fears and their dreams so that together, we can create a bright financial future that will ultimately offer greater peace of mind.

If you are feeling overwhelmed by the variety of products out there, if you are confused about what investment strategy works best for you, or if you want financial security and abundance for yourself and your family but just don't know where to start, this book was designed to be a beacon through the fog.

Every year, we help people just like you. We will listen, ask questions and explain your options. This includes working closely with you to map out your goals and objectives, understand your risk profile, determine how much money you need, and explore what else you may need in order to build and protect your wealth.

From developing advanced financial strategies to building an effective plan, we're here for you at every step of the way—so you can feel good about your financial future.

PENSIONS ARE NOT ENOUGH

Many Canadians are under the honest but mistaken impression that their pension, social security benefits and modest but unfocused savings combined will be enough for them to live on during their retirement. The truth is, for most people, it's just not enough.

We are living longer today than ever before, sometimes 20 or 30 more years after retirement. A longer lifespan comes with its own special financial challenges. Your financial strategy must be robust enough to endure this new reality and last just as long as you do—and even longer if you also want to protect your family.

We not only help people understand their options and take control of their financial lives, but we also give them peace of mind about their biggest fears, concerns and risks.

Here are some of the most common worries that our clients have expressed (in ***bold italics***):

"I want to make sure I have enough income to maintain my current lifestyle into retirement."

One of the biggest fears our clients have is running out of money. It's more common than you think. If you help a couple of children through university, move to a more temperate climate and enjoy a few luxuries, you may very quickly see your nest egg shrink.

The fact is that when you are retired, you have more time to spend money than you have to earn it. That's why every single person needs to think about what kind of retirement they want to enjoy and strategically plan for it—ideally well before they leave the office for the last time.

For many people, planning for retirement doesn't come naturally. We all live busy lives that can put a strain on our pocketbooks. By the time you find yourself with money to direct toward savings, you may find yourself closer to retirement than you realize.

The shortened savings phase may mean that you

retire with less to begin with. Additionally, if you carry non-deductible debt into retirement in the form of mortgage debt or consumer debt, you may find yourself in a difficult financial situation.

Here's why paying off your debt, including your mortgage, is such an important part of your overall financial health into retirement: Imagine that you and your spouse pay $1,100 every month toward the $80,000 balance you have left on your mortgage. If you don't work toward reducing that debt, $1,100 of your income will be locked into that debt even after you stop working.

On the other hand, the sooner you pay down your mortgage debt, the sooner you can reallocate that $1,100 to disposable income—and that can go a long way toward paying the rest of your monthly expenses after you retire.

So, if you are five years away from retirement and have no consumer debt, your number one goal should be to pay down your mortgage because that frees up a large amount of money every month. In a sense, paying off your mortgage sooner is actually a form of savings.

If you don't have debt and you have some disposable income before you retire, maximizing your RRSPs can be an excellent way to boost savings and increase wealth. An RRSP is a Registered Retirement Savings Plan that in Canada allows you to deduct the premium from your taxable income.

As an example, if you are earning $80,000 a year and your top tax rate is 35 percent, putting $1,000 into your RRSP will result in a tax deduction of $350 from the Canada Revenue Agency (CRA).

Maximizing RRSPs will help you accumulate wealth and supplement your retirement. Those extra savings can be crucial, especially near the end of life.

As much as we may try to avoid thinking about the possibility, moving to a retirement home or long-term care facility is an expensive but necessary reality for many Canadians. If you don't plan ahead for that expense, it could easily fall on the shoulders of your children and their families.

After reviewing your situation, we can help you make a plan to pay off debts and also strategize about managing future costs in a purposeful and responsible way. A customized financial strategy will take into account the lifestyle you want to have and enjoy.

"I want to keep inflation from eroding my net worth."

Inflation is a quiet force that can destroy the purchasing power of currency and spoil your net worth. The real meaning of "core inflation" comes from the 1980s.

During that era, the US was keeping inflation numbers low because government benefits and pensions were indexed to core inflation. Alternatively, a high inflation rate would significantly increase government expenditures and costs, which they wished to avoid. Since the debt levels in the US government were high, keeping the inflation rate low made government borrowing and programs more affordable.

Not everyone realizes that core inflation does not reflect the real inflation that ordinary consumers see at the pumps or the grocery store, and this can have a huge impact on how well your investments perform.

We believe that some countries are still publishing inflation figures that are much lower than they actually are. "Core inflation" in Canada is usually reported at about 2% per year. This might be the case if, say, you already own your home, you don't have any debt and your children have moved out.

For many working adults with young families and monthly expenses for food, gas, school supplies, clothing and other household costs, the actual rate of inflation is more like 8%. So, if you are getting a return of 2-3% on your investments, then you are actually falling behind because your returns are not keeping pace with the actual rate of inflation.

If you are investing in Guaranteed Investment

Certificates (GICs), it might be reassuring that you are being guaranteed 100% of your original investment.

Consider the reality that if your GICs are generating a 3% return, and the inflation rate is running higher than that, then your GICs are actually yielding no return at all. You are in fact losing money because the dollars you invested will be worth less when you take them out compared to when you first put them in.

In order to get any real benefit from your investments, they must yield a return that is greater than inflation. Over a 10 year period, a 2-3% inflation rate will need investments that yield 20-30% more income once redeemed if there is any money to be made. If the actual interest rate is closer to 8%, multiplying that by 10 years means you would need investments that yield 80%.

When trying to figure out what your net worth will really look like 20 or 30 years from now, it's important to make informed decisions about which investments will make your money work hard for you. We're here to help.

"I want to minimize the tax paid on my estate so I can pass my wealth on to my heirs."

We respect the amount of work you've put into building your wealth. We also know that for many of our clients, leaving their wealth to their heirs is a priority.

As with many things in life, minimizing taxes is easier said than done. There are so many interrelated issues to consider such as your own financial security in retirement, your assets and their potential to increase or decrease in value over time, and other factors.

Having a clear and comprehensive understanding of your financial situation and goals is the key to creating a plan that maximizes the amount you can pass on to your heirs. That is one of our top priorities.

Over the years, we have developed a simple and

effective tool that can help with that. Our Total Life Strategies Program will lay the groundwork that will not only help ensure that you have enough money to retire in comfort, but that your heirs will have enough to live active lives now and in the future.

In short, we can help you develop a plan that minimizes the taxes on your estate so that your money goes exactly where you want it to go: in the hands of your heirs.

One of the benefits of the Total Life Strategies Program is that it provides a framework for you to consider many parts of your life that will have an impact on your financial future. Having that information at your fingertips will help you and your financial advisor make informed decisions about not just what to do, but when and how to do it.

For example, if a couple is thinking of transferring their cottage to their children, it may be more beneficial to transfer the cottage now rather than wait 20 or 30 years. Decades from now, the market value of the cottage will have increased and so will the capital gains tax.

Of course, we may suggest something different if that couple needs to rely on the potential income from selling the cottage to fund their own retirement. Their risk tolerance and other circumstances must also be factored within the bigger picture.

Whether you are considering the consequences of a long post-retirement life, the impact of inflation on your investments, or the right strategy to maximize transfers to heirs, it takes knowledge, planning and discipline to create a plan that endures.

That's where our experience becomes your advantage. We're here to help you build your plan from the ground up. We can offer the customizable convenience of the Total Life Strategies Program. From the very beginning and for years to come, we want you to feel more confident that your wealth will be protected.

THE RISKS OF DO-IT-YOURSELF INVESTING

If you type "how to invest" into an on-line search engine, don't be surprised if you get at least 283,000,000 results. To put that into perspective, assuming you spend just one minute on each result, it would take you 3,275 days or almost nine years to read through it all.

If the sheer quantity of information makes your head spin, consider this: the Internet is the great equalizer. Anyone with access to a computer, tablet or mobile device can claim to know the secret to low-risk, high-reward ventures. They may even dazzle you with a slick website.

Maybe you're good at managing your budget, savings and cash flow. You may know that you don't know *everything* about investing, but you figure you know enough to get started.

Perhaps you've considered investing your money based on what has worked for others. You may have read books on the subject and consulted financial blogs. Maybe you pay close attention to the business section of the newspaper.

If you feel that your research has informed you enough to put a little money into exchange-traded funds (ETFs), or stocks that you've read up on and selected yourself, you might already be thinking of how much money you'll save on fees.

But beware—on-line and traditional media may not have all the answers about future risks and costs.

In the modern world of 24/7 news cycles, on-the-ground reporting and talking-head television, we are constantly inundated with opinions, options and apparent opportunities.

In many cases, the news has become more entertainment than fact. Social media platforms are no better. How many times has "big news" come out on social media only to be disputed or disproven seconds later?

Media makes us want to watch. It can implicitly

draw out and deepen our anxieties while continually reinforcing a sense of uncertainty within us. We learn to manage that anxiety by making decisions and taking actions that we think (or are told) will make us feel better.

Possibly worst of all, the urgency it manufactures within us may entice us to forgo our usual sense of caution and jump into something that we haven't fully investigated or thought through.

The last thing any of us wants is to miss out on an "opportunity of a lifetime." One of the fads in the media today is do-it-yourself investing. All too often, people get lured into the idea because the media says it's easy. The truth is, it's not—at least it's not easy to do it well.

If you rely on the media to tell you how, how much and when to invest, chances are you'll fall victim to the bright lights and fancy graphics of what is essentially an empty and unforgiving art form.

Let's take mutual funds as an example. In Canada,

there are over 16,000 mutual funds to choose from. Do you really have the time to study them all in detail? Which mutual funds match your risk profile and how will you decide whether to buy more or get out?

Since the financial world is always changing, are you committed to keeping yourself up-to-date not only about the mutual funds you have chosen but also the mutual funds you have not? Do you know exactly when and how to change course? What about next month or a year from now? Are you ready to dive in and fully commit yourself?

Even if you take the plunge and start investing on your own, where, exactly, are you going and how will you get there? Have you taken the time to make a plan?

Even the most informed, money-savvy people would likely have to spend an enormous amount of time and energy in order to invest their money wisely and responsibly. There must be an easier way to do something so 'easy.'

To be fair, some people who choose do-it-yourself investing think it will save them money in management fees, and for the true solo investor, they're right. If you buy an ETF entirely on your own accord, the management fee would be between 0.25% and 0.85%. That's great, providing you don't need to consult a professional for advice or support—ever.

Once you approach a stockbroker to do some of the research and you purchase your ETF through them, you might be looking at an additional 1% to 1.5% annual service fee. Now you're closing in on the 2% management fee that we often quote our clients.

Add to that the costs incurred if you're on your own and your investments get into trouble 10 years from now when market conditions have changed.

Depending on whether you've continued to invest hours tracking the bigger picture, you might hire a consultant to bail you out—and you know that won't come cheap.

Can you literally afford the risk of staying on top of your investments day after day and year after year?

Now let's consider penny stocks, which can seem like an accessible way to venture into the world of do-it-yourself investing. If you're lucky, investing a little while the stock is low could lead to big returns.

The trouble with penny stocks is that they are usually sold through a boiler room, which will usually sell them at a certain price. The boiler room can drive up the price in the short-term, making you think you have made a lot of money. They raise the price just enough to keep investors happy and eager to put more money into the stock.

When you decide to sell, the people in the boiler room might say that they are not buying the shares back right now, and before long they will fall off the radar with your money in their pocket.

Some people do get lucky with their first penny stock investment. The quick success can make the once cautious investor feel like a pro. It's in the second round of investing where people tend to get burned. When it comes to penny stocks or mutual funds, investing in either without doing the proper research is like taking your chances at a casino with a thousand tables.

Above and beyond penny stocks and mutual funds, just think about all the other options out there: RRSPs, RESPs, RDSPs, TFSAs, REITs, ETFs, GICs, Fixed Income Securities and Equities—and we're just scratching the surface. Each one has its own set of rules and tax implications.

Why in the world would you risk something as important as your   financial future without an experienced professional—someone who does this for a living day after day—by your side?

Working with a Certified Financial Planner can save your time, your money and your sanity. One of the major differences between risking it alone and partnering with an expert is that we can act as your steady and trustworthy source of information and advice. You'll see the difference from the moment you walk through the door.

We are aware of—but not necessarily swayed by— the latest investment trends on the news. We are focused on what gets results. We'll take the time to get to know you, discuss potential strategies and answer your questions. We'll work with you to build a solid plan moving forward.

We'll be there when we finalize the course of action and purchase the products, and we'll be there to monitor your account. We'll meet regularly with you to offer the latest information and advice, and we'll make adjustments as necessary. We become partners in your overall financial health. Can you really expect that kind of service and dedication from a website or a newspaper article?

To the prospective client who is a bit nervous about the future and who wants to put a financial plan together but isn't sure where to start, we are here for you. Be aware that there will always be uncertainties and unknowns, but you don't have to feel paralyzed by them. We have tools such as the Total Life Strategies Program to help demystify the process and equip you with a road map.

It is important not to take just any action, but *constructive* action that is measureable and has been proven over time. We'll work with you to develop a plan that is realistic and achievable. We'll help you understand your risk profile and design the plan around it.

Take comfort in knowing that you are always in control and we are there to help and guide you every step of the way.

FINDING A CERTIFIED FINANCIAL PLANNER YOU CAN TRUST

You're ready to invest and you're ready to benefit from the added value of working directly with an experienced financial planner.

Remember that the vast majority of financial planners will have roughly the same qualifications and varying amounts of experience. But what separates a good one from a great one?

The short answer is synergy. Never underestimate the value of trust in the context of selecting a financial professional. With so much at stake and so much to gain, feeling that trust—or synergy—is a critical part of a successful long-term relationship between a client and a financial planner.

At first, it can be challenging to know what to look for, what to ask and what to say to determine whether that synergy exists.

One way to gauge synergy is to analyze how the financial advisor interacts with you. Great financial planners actually listen. They don't try to overwhelm new clients with statistics, impress you by spouting off new products, or enthusiastically promise great rates of return.

The truly remarkable financial professionals do more listening than talking—that's how you know that they are really there for you.

Another way to gauge synergy is to pay attention to how comfortable you feel sharing details about your financial situation. Every financial advisor should ask you questions about your money, savings, debts and goals.

Pay close attention to how you feel when they ask you these kinds of questions. How easy is it for you to be completely forthright and comfortable answering them?

If you hesitate to share certain details, perhaps it's a sign that the synergy is not quite as strong as it could be.

Sometimes it's the client who feels the lack of

synergy; sometimes it's the advisor. Either way, if it's not a good fit, it's time to move on.

No matter how receptive the financial advisor is, and no matter how comfortable you feel, the synergy may not appear right away. As with most relationships, it develops best over time. Go with your gut.

Relationships are the heart and soul of our business. Every single client we have matters to us, and we will go out of our way to show them that we are ready and willing to support them over the long term—even for the little things that crop up along the way.

To give you an example, a client called us for advice about her car. Her vehicle was only four years old but it had a significant amount of mileage on it. The dealership was offering her an extended warranty but she wasn't sure if it made good financial sense to take the deal. We crunched some numbers and advised her that it would actually be cheaper for her to trade in her old car and lease a new car than it would be to pay for the warranty.

Over the years, we have seen our role grow from typical advisor to coach and mentor. Our job is not only to inform you of potential risks and benefits of options, but to warn you against taking actions that may be motivated by emotion rather than sound financial principles.

For instance, a potential client came to us asking for advice about how to invest a sum of money. When we asked a few more questions, she revealed that the money was the result of a leverage investment. In essence, she had borrowed the money she wanted to invest.

When we looked at the portfolio, it was very obvious that there were fairly high fees involved and that she was at serious risk should the market begin to fall.

We expressed our concerns about the high fees and explained the risks. We then recommended that she liquidate her loan, pay out the investment and get out of that arrangement. She was very grateful for our honest advice and followed through.

Whether you are a potential or existing client, if we can offer our expertise to help you make smart decisions, we will gladly answer the call. We know that building trusting, respectful relationships makes all the difference—and that's where we excel.

What also distinguishes us is that we don't want to grow into a huge company. Instead, we would prefer to focus on ensuring we can continue to give each and every client the personalized level of service they deserve.

As a direct result, we will accept only a small number of new clients every year. We want to get to know you, your family and how you picture your life going forward. We want to feel synergy with you and we want you to feel synergy with us.

It is both gratifying and humbling when a client remarks that he or she has been with us for 10, 20 or 30 years. We value our clients and consider a referral to be the biggest compliment we could receive. We are especially delighted when we are privileged to work with the son or daughter of a client—that is a true indication of trust.

When you make a commitment to partner with us as a client, we also make a commitment to partner with you. Our clients don't just stay with us because of the returns we get for them, but also because of the way we work together. Communication with our clients and within our interdisciplinary team is a key part of our success and your peace of mind.

As a new client, you will sit with one of the senior members of our team to discuss many aspects of your life. We'll talk about your current financial situation and start getting a sense of how you picture your financial future. We will almost always meet our clients more frequently in the beginning so we can lay the groundwork for the road ahead.

Once we have discussed the foundation of the plan and agreed on a path forward, we'll put the plan in place. After the initial set-up, we will usually recommend meeting in person either quarterly or bi-annually depending on your preferences.

Over time, many of our clients elect to skip a scheduled meeting because they feel a certain level of comfort with us handling their portfolio and they see no reason to deviate from the current plan.

Most of our clients live locally, but we have also had the pleasure of doing business with people who live farther away.

We are licensed in Ontario, Québec and a number of other provinces, and many of our clients refer their out-of-town friends and relatives to us.

Like any client, we would ask you to come see us in person for the initial interview so we can meet and build the financial plan.

Once everything is set up, we can then communicate via telephone, e-mail or Skype—whichever you prefer. We can also scan and e-mail documents for your signature.

Integrating secured technologies makes it easy and convenient to work with us.

Should you have a question between scheduled meetings, we invite you to call our office. Very often questions can be answered immediately by our policy service team.

If for some reason it can't, a more senior member of our team will usually take the call right away. If they are unavailable, you can expect a call from us within 24 hours.

Being accessible to our clients is one way we foster trust—and to us, trust is everything.

THE FIRST MEETINGS

We are generalists of many specific options, not specialists of one option that is being pushed on us to promote or sell. That means we help individuals and families reach their retirement goals by understanding the entire landscape of choices available to them and weeding out the strategies and products that don't suit your vision for your future.

What's left are well-researched opportunities that will not only protect your wealth, but help it grow healthier and stronger.

Our typical client is a person or couple who wants to retire in comfort or is already retired and has $500,000 or more to invest. They may wish to explore how to pay less tax, protect their family and their estate, or invest in their children or grandchildren's financial future and well-being. If this sounds like you, we have the expertise, experience and resources to help you protect what and whom you value most.

If for any reason we do not have the right synergy, we will connect you to other trusted financial planners at a different branch who might suit your needs better than we can.

We are selective of our family of clients for two reasons: we find that being selective produces better overall satisfaction and we find that being selective also gives us the means to devote more time to individuals and families with whom we have more synergy.

Over the next several years, our growth as a business will be careful and measured. We do not want to be bogged down with a huge number of clients. In fact, we envision adding only five or six new clients each year so we can continue to offer the highly personalized service that has distinguished us from other institutions.

When we say we want to meet with you, get to know you and offer you solid, personalized advice, we are focused on delivering on these commitments.

One question we often ask during the first meeting tends to surprise our clients: "What do you expect of us?" It may seem strange, but it's an excellent way to help determine if you understand what we do and if we're likely to be a good fit over the long term.

For example, if your answer to this question is a variation on, "I want you to be able to buy individual stocks," or "When I call, I want you to buy the stocks that I want to purchase," then we know right away that we are not a good fit because we are not licensed to buy individual stocks.

Similarly, if your answer to "What do you expect of me?" is something like "I expect you to call me and warn me to get out of the market before there is an economic downturn," then we are not the right financial advisors for you. We cannot time the market, and saying or implying that we could would be disingenuous and just plain wrong.

If you tell us that you are looking for us to give you sound advice that can help you protect and grow your finances, investments, savings and quality of life, then we'd likely be starting on the right foot.

Similarly, if you need advice about long-term financial planning investments and help weighing risks and rewards, we are there for you.

If your personal or work circumstances have changed—whether you've received a severance, pension rollover or legal settlement—we can show you how to make that money work harder for you.

And, if you're looking for a personalized, customized financial plan to take you step by step through the rest of your working and retirement years, we have one-of-a-kind products like the Total Life Strategies Program to offer.

Asking about your expectations of us early in the relationship is a benefit to you because it reduces the chances of a fundamental misunderstanding about what we do, what we don't do, and how we go about managing your account.

Now let's get more specific: We are licensed to sell

life insurance, GICs, mutual funds and segregated funds. We'll shop around for options that are the best possible fit for your unique circumstances.

All of our solutions, including those that reduce taxes for clients, are fully sanctioned by the Canada Revenue Agency.

Absolutely everything we sell, all the advice we give and all the methods we use are designed to take advantage of existing tax rules. Our honesty is your peace of mind.

Here's what we do *not* offer: We don't offer individual stocks, nor do we sell securities that are offered by stockbrokers. We offer advice on life insurance and disability coverage, but we do not look after comprehensive car insurance, house insurance or commercial coverage.

Finally, we do not offer our clients legal advice. We have a strong working relationship with several local legal professionals and will happily refer our clients to them as needed.

In addition, our clients occasionally benefit from the expertise of other professionals such as accountants. If you need assistance beyond the scope of what we can offer, we will refer you to a trusted professional.

If you become our client, our first meetings together will have already set the groundwork for a trustworthy working relationship. Our process follows the pattern below.

Conduct a needs analysis: Through a series of personal interviews, we'll work with you to better understand your needs, personal goals, time horizon and risk tolerance.

Analyze asset allocation: Having the proper mix of equities, bonds and cash will determine the potential risk and return of your portfolio (i.e. asset allocation). We use sophisticated analysis tools to find the right mix.

Build your wealth plan: A wealth plan factors your current assets, planned contributions prior to retirement and expected withdrawals after retirement. We then illustrate the investment strategy (i.e. asset allocation to balance risk versus reward) to project your return and estimate future values of your portfolio.

Access investment managers whom we, as your financial planners, will liaise with on your behalf: Our wealth optimization process simplifies the maze of investment products and suppliers by focusing on finding the most reliable investment managers. These experts will be directly managing the financial products we've recommended for you so "who" will be managing them is just as important as "what" you are purchasing.

Implement the strategy: Once we fully understand your needs and together have agreed on a "road map" that will move us in the direction of your goals, we will begin the process of implementing your strategy.

Monitor your progress: We will monitor your progress through regular reviews of your portfolio and meet with you at regularly scheduled intervals to discuss progress.

Rebalance your portfolio: Market cycles cause different asset categories to do well at different times. Rebalancing brings your portfolio back to the original asset mix at regular intervals to take advantage of these cycles.

Whether you are looking for a long-term financial plan, a check-up or a second opinion, we have the expertise and experience to help you retire in comfort and feel secure about your financial future.

HOW WE ARE DIFFERENT FROM A BANK

One of the most common questions potential clients ask us is how we are different from a bank. It's a very good question.

We offer our clients a full range of financial products and solutions. Unlike a bank that is limited to offering products specific to its brand, we have the freedom to search for a variety of diverse products from a variety of suppliers.

Once we truly understand your profile and goals, we will investigate and narrow down the most suitable options to meet your unique needs.

Think of it this way: using a bank for financial products is like going to a fast-food restaurant chain. If you are hungry for a burger and fries, most of the items on the menu and the way the food tastes will be standard fare.

If, however, you are on a special diet, you wish they could prepare your food a bit differently or you just want more choices, all the fast food restaurant can offer you is, well, their standard menu because that's all it's allowed to sell.

Now think of us this way: working with us is like going through a restaurant referral service when you know you want something unique but aren't quite sure what to try.

To continue with this analogy, we'll ask you about what you like and don't like, what your cravings and food restrictions are, who will be joining you, and what you want to take away from this experience.

We will then search high and low for 'restaurants' that can offer the flavours, flexibility and level of service that will meet your expectations.

Another thing you will get from us is highly attentive, personalized service. You will be dealing with a family business and familiar faces from year to year. Our limited client list and measured expansion gives us ample time to learn about each of our clients so that we can build a careful, customized plan just for you.

The value we add is that we work hard to understand what you are trying to achieve, develop a plan, choose the right investments to match the profile, and then monitor it regularly.

We believe that success for our clients is largely the result of the effort and care that we put into each one of our interactions, especially at the start of the relationship when trust is beginning to take shape.

Explaining how we get paid in a complete and straightforward way is another important part of earning your trust. If you don't ask us directly during our first meeting, we will raise the topic ourselves.

As an investor, it's important that you understand all the details, including what fees you will be paying, before you invest.

Sales charges and other fees may apply depending on which investments you choose, how and when you buy them, and what accounts you hold them in.

Keep in mind that although you may not pay fund expenses directly, these charges will still reduce the return you get on your investment. When you're investing thousands of dollars, not taking the time to understand your options could become costly.

We believe in being open and transparent from the start, so that you know what to expect and why we might recommend certain options over others.

To give you a general idea as to how fees work, here is an overview of four common types of sales charges associated with mutual funds:

Front-end load or initial sales charge: Some mutual funds charge a fee up front. The fee comes out of the sum of money you wish to invest in the fund.

For example, if you want to invest $100,000 in a mutual fund with a front-end load of 2%, $2,000 would be paid toward the fee and $98,000 would be invested.

Back-end load or deferred sales charge: Some mutual funds charge a fee when you sell your units or shares. The longer you keep a fund with a back-end load, the less you'll be charged when you sell it. The fee decreases every year according to a fixed schedule.

If you hold the mutual fund long enough, the fee may decrease to zero and you won't have to pay a fee when you sell. Some fund companies may also let you take some of your money (usually 10%) out of the fund each year without charging a fee.

In this case, the advisor receives commission up front from the mutual fund company when you buy the fund. Any deferred sales charge you pay goes to the mutual fund company.

For example, if you invested $100,000 in several mutual funds, the full $100,000 would be invested and each year the fund company would withdraw their management fee from your account. When you receive your statement, the net return shown is the return on your investment after the fee has been withdrawn. The management fee comes out every year whether you have a gain or a loss.

Low load or low sales charge: Low load funds tend to carry a lower sales charge when you buy your units or shares, and a lower redemption fee when you sell them. You usually won't have to pay a redemption fee if you hold your units or shares for a certain amount of time.

No load – A no load fund has no commission fees up front associated with it when you buy or sell. Be aware that a no load fund may not always be a better deal than a load fund. Be sure to compare the performance of each fund and how well it fits your investment profile before you decide to proceed.

The management fee that goes to the mutual fund company is compensation for the overall management of the fund.

In other words, the fee pays for professional managers who buy and sell various stocks, and their expertise is designed to give you returns on your money. The portion that we receive as financial advisors is compensation for managing your account, keeping it up to date and reviewing it with you on a regular basis.

In the case of segregated funds, which allow you to name beneficiaries in the contract to avoid probate fees on death, and also provide a guarantee of capital on death, the same front end, back end, low or no load options apply.

If we happen to recommend Guaranteed Investment Certificates or GICs (which we generally don't if the actual rate of inflation is higher than the certificate's guaranteed rate of return), we would typically get about 0.2% of the investment. For example, if you invested $10,000, we would be compensated $20.

The compensation we get for life insurance is straightforward and standard practice: we generally get a commission up front and it is typically equivalent to the amount of the first annual premium. For example, if you purchase personal life insurance for a 20-year term where the total annual premium is locked in at $300 per year for 20 years or $25 per month, we would be paid $300.

All in all, many of our clients agree that the expert advice and trusted experience that a financial advisor provides an investor is well worth the management fees.

Hiring a stockbroker may seem like a legitimate way to avoid paying fees, but take heed of the drawbacks of such an arrangement. Stockbrokers charge transactional fees for buying and selling stocks. In addition, a 1%-1.5% fee may be charged annually for monitoring your account.

A stockbroker may assist you in selecting a portfolio and monitor it for you over time, but advice and ongoing service often carries an additional fee that you must negotiate with your stockbroker.

By investing through us, you'll get personal service, ongoing access to advice that is specific to your situation and continued monitoring of your account. We'll meet with you regularly to discuss your portfolio's performance and make changes as needed.

We're always here to answer questions, particularly if your circumstances change or you are facing a major decision that could impact your financial well-being.

In our experience, this is the kind of attention and expertise that adds value to an investor's experience, protects against costly mistakes and grows wealth over the long term.

CREATING AN INVESTMENT PLAN

By now, we hope that you are familiar with how we operate. We work with clients who are typically nearing retirement or newly retired and have at least $500,000 to invest.

We selectively grow our client base so we can continue to offer personalized service, a customized plan, and ongoing advice and support. We value and are dedicated to building a long-term relationship based on synergy.

If this sounds like a relationship you can entrust with your financial future, it's time to discuss the specifics of creating an investment plan.

Clients often ask us when they should start investing. Most experts agree that the earlier a person starts investing, the easier it is.

Putting away small amounts early in your adult life will put you on the right track toward finding financial freedom sooner in life. However, if you see retirement on the horizon and haven't started saving yet, it's not too late. We can still build a plan for you that will benefit you in the future.

If you are approaching retirement and have existing non-deductible debt, we often recommend that the first thing to do is to take active steps to eliminate it. Debt can include credit card balances, car payments and your mortgage(s).

Second, we usually recommend maximizing your contributions to Registered Savings Plans like RRSPs because they allow you to deduct the premium from your taxable income and help supplement your income when you do retire.

Third, we usually recommend scrutinizing your monthly budget—if you even have one. Do you know how much you spend on groceries every month? How many coffees or lunches have you purchased this past week and what was the total cost?

Are you paying interest, fees, penalties and subscriptions that you may not even be aware of?

Are you paying the best rates for household services and other essential expenditures?

Many people just don't know how much they are spending every month. If you find that you have very little money left over after paying your expenses each month, it will likely be very difficult for you to maintain your current standard of living when your income decreases during retirement. It may be time to cut down on non-essential spending in order to direct the extra money into a focused savings plan.

If the information shows that the amount spent equals the amount earned, it is important to realize that retirement may not be a reality until the spending is in order.

Once most—if not all—non-deductible debt is paid off and spending is in check, it is time to start building your plan. To get you started—and this is what truly sets us apart from any other financial institution—we will invite you to participate in our Total Life Strategies Program.

The aims of this proprietary program are to learn more about you, your current situation and your vision of the future; to gauge how clearly you see your future in its present form; and to help you focus on what action we can take together in order to achieve that vision.

All of the information you provide will help both of us in our journey together. It will help you set priorities and outline the road ahead. It will also help us determine how we can best help you achieve your dreams.

Some clients find this phase challenging. If you do not have a good sense of either your current situation or where you want to end up, it can be difficult to provide answers to the level of detail that is necessary for moving ahead. It may feel like drawing a map to an unknown or unclear destination.

If you're not sure where you are now and where you want to go just yet, please don't despair. We are here to help you draw the map. We'll ask lots of questions and help you consider your options. Just give us a sense of where you might want to go and we'll help you get there. Even if you simply know where you don't want to go, we can help with the process of elimination until a general direction begins to emerge.

Once we both understand what your goals are, it's time to decide how to get there. The plan we recommend for you will depend on your own particular circumstances, risk profile and priorities. We know that no two clients will use exactly the same road to get to their destination. That's why we build a completely customized plan just for you.

What matters most to you? For example, if you would like to donate some of your wealth to charity or a religious organization, we can certainly accommodate that.

Similarly, we can build a plan that gifts an amount of money or assets you specify to your adult children or grandchildren. We would discuss related issues like capital gains taxes on any gifts before we proceed, but in some cases, gifting assets this way makes smart financial sense.

As another example, gifting an asset to children could be a very big benefit for a widow or widower who, after the death of a spouse, had all the income for the family in their name.

Taking no action would probably mean that the income would be taxed at the highest marginal tax rate. If that income was derived from investments, then the surviving spouse would be paying high tax on the return.

So instead of having a lot of taxable income today, the spouse could gift that income to the children, thereby lowering the spouse's tax bracket and reducing the amount of tax that the spouse would have to pay.

Gifting assets to lower the amount of taxes owing is just one consideration. Drafting a will is another. A will is a very important part of your overall financial and investment plan, especially when you have assets, property and dependents to think about. Far too many people neglect to make a will, and that's a trend that we would like to see change.

A will is more complex than most people realize because the succession plan can affect a variety of other issues like capital gains taxes. It is critically important to become well-informed about your options as they relate to succession planning and the full range of outcomes for potential courses of action.

Unfortunately we cannot dispense legal advice about wills or any other subject to our clients because we are not lawyers. We can, however, work closely with lawyers on your behalf before making a recommendation.

Our strategy for succession planning is to keep things as simple as possible. An average family with a home, a cottage and some investments may only need a very simple will that outlines a relatively straightforward succession plan.

If your situation requires a more intricate plan, we will partner with experienced legal professionals to get it done. No matter the complexity of your succession plan, our job is to look at your assets and minimize taxes wherever possible using the vehicles available to us.

Another often overlooked part of a succession plan is powers of attorney. A power of attorney is a trusted person whom you designate to handle your affairs if you ever lose the capacity to do so yourself.

There are two kinds of powers of attorney in Ontario: one for financial affairs and one for medical decisions. One person can hold both powers, but many people select a different person for each.

Putting someone you trust in that role—even if they don't have to assume it for 20 or 30 years (or never)—is often a wise decision. Plus, knowing that someone you trust will manage your affairs on your behalf can give you greater peace of mind.

Getting back to your core investments, we will spend the time discovering what kind of investor you are. If, based on our conversations and the answers you provide during the Total Life Strategies Program, we determine that you are a relatively conservative investor but you do want growth, we will usually recommend an appropriate combination of stocks and bonds to meet your objectives.

We may recommend a different mix of stocks and bonds if you are comfortable with and can afford to take that risk.

Once we determine the right ratio for you, we'll select an array of funds. The number of mutual funds in any one portfolio can depend on the investor, but we will ensure that the funds we select will provide sufficient diversification.

As a point of interest, mutual funds are usually recommended over individual stocks, ETFs or index funds. In our experience, mutual funds tend to offer a smoother investment experience because there are seasoned managers who have a lot of research and expertise at hand to make sure that your lows are not as low—although this also means that your highs may not be as high. Mutual funds are a good option for clients who prefer less volatility overall.

Following our first meetings, we will have had the chance to get to know you, your current situation, your goals, priorities and concerns. We will have relayed that information back to you as we understand it, and we will have used that information to draw up a customized and detailed plan moving forward. You will also have had a chance to review the plan and decide if you want to proceed.

With your approval, the next step is to sign documents that authorize us to transfer your investments to our firm. You officially become our client at this point and we will then move forward with the investment plan we discussed.

We often defer non-pressing matters to our quarterly meetings. Succession plans or eventual sale of an asset like a cottage may best be discussed at a later date. Keeping us abreast of your priorities or any changing circumstances will help us prioritize our discussions.

TRUST OVER TIME

As Alexander Graham Bell famously said, "Before anything else, preparation is the key to success." The work you put in to the preparation phase of your financial plan not only makes it much easier to manage your portfolio wisely over time, but also offers a greater peace of mind.

We strive to build a proper mix in your portfolio from the outset so that you feel at ease and don't have an overwhelming urge to constantly make changes to your account.

We will review the various performances with you at our quarterly or semi-annual meetings. If there are changes that need to be made, we will make them.

If there are no changes, we'll just carry on with the same mix that we had in the previous quarter. It is recommended that funds not be moved around a lot; rather, it is important to build a portfolio properly at the beginning and then allow it to grow.

As an example, we had a client who recently retired at the age of 62. One day he asked, "Shouldn't we change the mix in my portfolio to something more conservative?"

We suggested staying the course. First of all, he was in his mid-sixty's and fit as a fiddle. Since he could easily need to rely on that investment for another 30 years, the wisest course of action for him was to let the equity side of his investments grow over time and take his income from the bond side.

If a portfolio is built properly from the beginning, there is less need for it to be adjusted over time.

That's not to say that your portfolio should *never* change, but the changes must be done for the right reasons and in the right way.

Through the years, it has been our experience not to hear from our clients all that often during smooth periods when the markets are doing well. When there is a sudden and steep downturn like the one we went through in 2008, many of our clients called us in a panic telling us to make drastic changes to their accounts. Our biggest job then, as it is now, was to keep our clients on track.

We understand the anxiety that accompanies a sudden drop in the market. We try to prevent our clients from making sudden moves that are driven by emotion, because in our experience, if a decision is driven by emotion, it is often the wrong one.

We've sat down with many anxious clients and told them that they should hold off from making any big changes right now because, given time, the market will come back and will do well for us.

Here's some proof: If we look back at the more than 200 clients who have been with us for the last 25 years, we will notice an interesting trend: Our clients have still averaged an increase in returns since and including 2008.

(Note: This is not an indication or guarantee of future performance or promise in returns.)

Refraining from making financial decisions fuelled

by emotion is a hard message for some to hear. As your financial advisors, we are here to help you make the best financial decisions for you based on logic and evidence. With us as your advisors through thick and thin, we can help you achieve long-term financial stability and overall peace of mind.

We are confident in giving this advice because we have experienced the market downturns of 1987, 1998, 2000 and 2008. Seeing the stock market dropping 20% or 30% were indeed very scary times—but being scared is never a good reason on its own to make huge changes, especially if you already have the proper mix and good value in your portfolios.

Despite this, we remind our clients that we don't know how to time markets. We have never been proven successful at it, and we have never known anybody who has been.

We will not be able to tell you when the next downturn will be, but we can tell you this: If we are invested in good value stocks and bonds, we will likely weather the storm very well by simply holding fast and potentially adding to your existing investment when the market is down. An unreasonably sharp sell-off is always an opportunity to purchase at a discount. Put your trust in our experience and our long track record of success.

Here's another reason you can trust our advice: the investments we offer our own clients are the same investments into which we put our own personal money.

Investing is a very personal choice that we will help you make once we know what kind of investor you are and what goals you want to achieve before, during and after retirement. We are committed to helping you create a bright future for yourself and your family for years to come.

With trust and respect at its core, consistency is another key part of our business. Some of our clients inquire about when I intend to retire and what will happen to their account when I do. I'd like to assure you that I intend to continue working for at least the next 10 years.

As I approach retirement and gradually cut back my own hours, I will begin to phase in a financial planner with whom I have good synergy and begin to introduce him or her to our clients to see if they feel the same way. We will listen to our clients and encourage them to provide honest feedback.

It's so important to me that our clients continue to feel like they can truly count on the advice and support they are getting from us. Of course, you always have the option to find a financial planner on your own. Either way, once a good match has been made, we will turn over your file to whomever you choose. Our goal is to make the transition as smooth as possible.

Some of our clients have even asked us how we might maintain consistently high standards if one of us were to suddenly pass away or otherwise become unable to continue managing our accounts. We understand that consistency is an important part of a trusting relationship between client and advisor, so the question is a fair one.

My wife and full partner in the firm, Joyce Owen, would be fully capable of assuming my accounts—and vice versa.

Should you prefer another solution, we would be pleased to call on one of the capable and trusted members in our professional network to take on your account. Our staff would work closely to make the transition as fast and seamless as possible.

All of our efforts are for the same end: consistency in service, knowledge and performance. Making sure that our clients are well cared for even after our partnership ends is one of our top priorities.

TOTAL LIFE STRATEGIES PROGRAM

Throughout this book, it has been emphasized that unless you are an industry expert, trying to choose and manage multiple investments and financial products by yourself can put your financial future at risk.

In addition, getting advice from someone (or something) that doesn't have the expertise and experience to customize an investment plan for you is also risky. Can you afford to take those chances?

While you may understand and even agree with the need to get expert advice you can trust, you may still find yourself struggling with not knowing where to begin. How, exactly, can you drill down to what you really want out of life once you're ready to make a plan?

Maybe you're not sure what you can and can't afford in retirement, let alone *when* you want to retire. Perhaps you've been spending so much time living in the moment that you haven't even begun to think about your retirement. It's possible you have already put a lot of thought into what you want and don't want—you have a dream and money saved—but you're not quite sure how to protect your wealth from future expenses, fees and taxes.

No matter your circumstances, we designed the Total Life Strategies Program for people just like you.

This program was designed to ask you all the right questions, sharpen your vision of your future and outline practical steps forward. Throughout and after the program, as our client, you'll have full access to our personalized advice and customized financial planning strategies.

The Total Life Strategies Program is much more than a questionnaire. It's a unique tool that is packed with pointed questions and exercises that will help you think about your goals, prioritize what is most important to you, and set out the specific actions you need to take to achieve them.

We will be challenging you to take the time to think, but we'll also be encouraging you to dream.

All the effort you put into the initial part of the Total Life Strategies Program will help set you and your family up for lasting peace of mind because you'll *know* that you have a solid plan that is tailored just for you.

To give you a sense of what to expect, the program begins with The Total Life Strategies Scorecard. This section sets out a series of questions such as whether you have a clear and well-defined vision of your future or whether you have a step-by-step action plan in place to achieve your goals.

There are scales from 1 – 10 and a final score to calculate. You'll be prompted to think deeply about why you gave yourself the scores you did and what you need to do to improve them. We'll follow up by discussing these results with you.

These and other exercises will demonstrate that a big part of making a plan is transferring your vision to paper. The Total Life Strategies Program is designed to help you gather your dreams and give them more real-world substance by writing them down. It's a small but crucial step toward solidifying your vision and making it a reality.

This vision statement will act as your True North. It will help ground you, give you confidence that you know where you are going, and help you get back on track if you lose your way.

Once you have a clear vision in mind, it's time to start defining your Investor Profile. We will ask questions to learn more about your: Time Horizon, Risk Tolerance, Current Income, Financial Stability and Level of Discretion. The Investor Profile provides you and your financial planner with an in-depth understanding of who you are as an investor.

After your Investor Profile has been created, we will then work on mapping out an Investor Profile Decision Grid to address the basic issues at heart of any sound investment strategy. The result is that the nature of the returns required, the tolerance for short term losses and the projected time horizon for a particular investment can be discovered. This, in turn, helps balance between return and downside risk.

Creating a detailed monthly budget is another exercise and I'll warn you in advance: it gets pretty detailed. From housing and food costs to childcare and health expenses, it really drills down to have a very close look at the spending patterns for your wants and needs.

If you've never done this before, even doing this once through our program will open your eyes like never before. We can get lost in the details of life. Getting lost in the dollars of life is what can truly cost us from month to month and year to year.

So many of us have heard about how cutting out one purchased coffee per day can save us hundreds per year. Where else is money leaking out of your wallet? We can guarantee you that if you don't already have a monthly budget where every dollar is tracked, simply going through the exercise even once will reveal areas where you can put dollars back into your pocket and dollars towards a brighter future.

Another benefit of the Total Life Strategies Program is that it provides helpful tips and a very practical document checklist to make sure no stone has been left unturned.

It is so thorough that you'll come away knowing your financial situation—from risks to opportunities—better than ever before.

Some of the questions we ask are specific. Some are open-ended and invite you to dream. The answers you give will help us select not only the right mix of investment products, but also the investment strategies that work best for your unique circumstances.

Once you complete the program, the outcome will be a totally personalized wealth plan that YOU understand just as well as we do.

Together, we will have:

- Clearly established your goals (both personal and financial)

- Discovered your risk profile

- Determined how much money you need to achieve your goals

- Figured out what else you need in addition to money to have greater peace of mind

If you'd like to learn more about how this program can help you reach your financial and personal goals, please contact us.

CONCLUSION

We live in an extraordinary time. Never before have we had so many opportunities for wealth, adventure and knowledge of the world around us. We have made huge leaps in science, medicine and technology—and yet there is so much more to discover.

Our modern world is full of wonders that my father could only dream about. We can connect to far-away family and friends with a click of a mouse, buy products without ever having seen them in real life and seek out billions of bits of information from the comfort of our homes. In some ways, life today has never been better.

Despite our advances, our global community and ever-changing economy can bring a new level of uncertainty. How you manage the uncertainty will play a big role in your overall happiness.

Some let the uncertainty overwhelm them to the point of helplessness. Others partner with trusted experts for support and take action. Which path will you choose?

We are here to tell you that you *can* take action. With our help, you can build a life plan based on solid, tried-and-true principles.

We get to know you and what you really want out of life. We work with you to build a one-of-a-kind plan that you can feel good about.

Once that plan is in place, you can enjoy the peace of mind that comes with knowing that we are always looking out for you.

You can finally stop worrying about money and start enjoying your life.

Just think about what freedom from financial worry would feel like.

With the future well mapped out, you can live in the present.

You can enjoy all the things that a full and happy life has to offer.

CONCLUSION

You can finally pursue your dreams.

Have the courage to take the first step and call us. We can help you protect the people you love, maximize your wealth and take control of your life.

CUSTOMER TESTIMONIAL

Testimonial

Are you looking for someone you can trust? who will give you unbiased advice? who will put your interests first? Do you prefer dealing directly with a friendly and personable individual, in a warm and sympathetic environment? Then, like me, you will turn to Charles Brophy and his Team at Brophy Financial Planning!

For almost twenty years, Charles and I have worked together. I have been able to assure my ongoing financial well-being, grow my assets, plan for the future, share great ideas and work towards realizing my philanthropic dreams, with the help of his expert personal guidance and his up to date knowledge of the market.

I have benefitted from regular and well planned financial planning meetings where we tailored needed actions to meet my goals. At Brophy Financial Planning, I have been warmly welcomed, made to feel at home among friends. I am so thankful that "Charlie and the Team" are there for me !

Marie A. Loyer

Dr. Marie A. Loyer

September 9, 2014

1 4 0 3 - 1 6 0 George St. Ottawa K1 N 9 M2

TAKE THE NEXT STEP...

Are you ready to start to get your finances in order, so that you can thrive in this present economy?

Are you ready to prepare for a brighter future?

Then take the next step and contact me for a FREE consultation, so that we can see how best to serve your needs. You can reach me using the contact details below.

Thank you again for the opportunity to serve you. I am looking forward to hearing from you.

Sincerely,

Charlie Brophy, CFP, ChFC, CLU
Financial Advisor
Brophy Financial Planning
Phone: (613) 728-9573
Email: charlie@brophyfinancial.com

ABOUT THE AUTHOR

Charles Brophy CFP, ChFC, CLU
Financial Advisor

Though he is officially Charles, his clients know him as Charlie. With thirty years of experience in financial, retirement and estate planning, Charlie always offers his clients a Secure, Measurable, Achievable. Responsible, Trustworthy (S.M.A.R.T.) approach to their finances.

Charlie stays S.M.A.R.T. by attending industry workshops and seminars. His knowledge of current market trends and conditions, combined with his many years of experience, means that Charlie always provides his clients with a very balanced perspective on the financial aspect of their lives.

Charles Brophy is a Certified Financial Planner (CFP), a Chartered Financial Consultant (ChFC) and a Chartered Life Underwriter (CLU).

Clients can count on Charlie to give expert advice with a personal touch. Whether you need help with financial, retirement or estate planning, Charlie will help you achieve your financial goals.

ABOUT PERISSOS MEDIA

CREATE your product.
BUILD your brand.
CONSTRUCT your platform.
BROADCAST your message.
EXPAND your reach and income...

Perissos Media helps business owners, speakers, consultants, professionals, sales teams, ministry leaders and inspired individuals to PUBLISH books, audio and video training products and other marketing materials, in order to BUILD your platform and ELEVATE you to Expert Status in your field—with all the financial and lifestyle benefits that come with it.

Even if you have never written or recorded a word, we have resources and services to help you get your message out, one step at a time.

For help in building or expanding your platform, and to publish your message to a greater audience, please visit:

www.IWantToPublish.com

We look forward to serving you,

Jerry Kuzma
Director
PerissosMedia.com